5 Steps to Beating the Trap

B. F. Nkrumah

Copyright © 2020 B. F. Nkrumah

All rights reserved.

ISBN: 9798623425881

www.BFNkrumah.com

CONTENTS

	Introduction	i
Step 1	Identifying your trap	1
Step 2	Becoming aware that there's more	29
Step 3	Recognize the changes that need to be made in you.	53
Step 4	Preparing when it's not your time.	79
Step 5	Confidence for my moment.	95

Introduction

First I would like to thank you for purchasing this book and congratulate you for desiring to beat the Traps in your life. Beating the Trap is something I've been practicing, learning or teaching for over fourteen years. I have gone through a total transformation in my life and I am still transforming and becoming better day by day. Along my journey it has become my desire to help others also live out their maximum potential and that is why I penned this book.

As you will hear me say over and over in this book, Beating the Trap is a process. This is not something where you read the book and immediately have all the answers. This is something that you will have to read slowly, internalize what you're reading and actually answer questions that are being asked. It is not my intention that you speed read through this book and tell the world that it is a great book. It is my desire that you take the time to process the principles I am teaching and drastically transform your life.

Throughout the book I have certain questions in bold fonts. These are questions I want you to stop and really think about. This book isn't that long so you could read it in one sitting but that is not the best way to see the results you want. As you come across these questions I want you to think about what you've read prior to it and actually take the time to answer them before you read on. I know most people won't but if you're serious about changing, you will use the book the right way.

Along with the questions in bold, after every chapter there is a checklist. The reason they are there is for you to actually go through each step I have on there, (and steps you come up with yourself) and do what each step tells you to do especially pertaining to writing things down. I recommend you get a journal to document all of your progress. When you get to the last chapter you will need to have everything written down to help you complete your process. This is not a book to just read; this is a book to work through.

It is my desire to give people the tools they need to succeed in life but what are tools without instructions on how to use them? These instructions I'm giving you are for your benefit. I know you probably have read a ton of motivational books; well this is not one. This is an equipping book. I'm not just trying to inspire you; I'm trying to show you how to do the work.

As you go through this book, take your time and allow the information to sink in. I pray you will successfully complete your process and end up Beating YOUR Trap.

Step 1
Identifying YOUR Trap

Do you want to live a life of **MORE?**

MORE money?

MORE vacations?

MORE time with family?

MORE meaningful relationships?

MORE control over your emotions?

MORE control over the fears that paralyze you?

MORE in tune with your internal greatness?

If you are like me and you want **MORE** out of life then there is only **ONE** question you need to answer.

WHAT IS HOLDING ME BACK?

Whatever is holding you back (and we're going to find it) that is your TRAP. That is what you have to beat.

You don't have to worry about competition. You don't have to worry about who's going to give you an opportunity, where the money is going to come from, how you're going to execute your plan or how you're going to completely transform your character etc. The only thing you have to do is identify and Beat Your Trap and everything else will fall in place.

Trap: any idea or belief that internal (i.e. thinking you're not good enough) or external (i.e. not having access to resources) factors can keep you where you are in life. These beliefs are usually a product of perception from failures, environment and or circumstance but they are always inaccurate.

One thing about life is we can grow up around so much BS that anything can become normal to us. The BS can be so normal that it causes us to become use to a lifestyle that we shouldn't. I know I grew up with so much pain in my life that I didn't even see it as pain any longer. It was just what was supposed to happen to me.

I guess this was my minds way of keeping itself from going crazy; just act like it doesn't matter and keep it moving. But what happens when the normality of the craziness you've seen all your life becomes a part of who you are? What happens is you begin to willingly live beneath your greatness because you subconsciously feel you can only be what you see every day and even though you can easily be **MORE**, you feel TRAPPED!

This TRAPPED mindset will go against all reason and really have you feeling like who you are, is all you can ever be. You'll think things like "people where I'm from don't make it to do that" or "people are going to look at my background and won't work with me" or "I can't get a loan" or "they were right, I'm never going to be able to change" or _____ insert what you tell yourself here.

All of these types of thoughts are what TRAP us. Notice, each of these thoughts will keep you from any and all action. If you truly believe these things, you will want MORE but never take any action to get it done and be TRAPPED right where you are.

The only way to "beat" something is to fight it. So right now I want you to peel back the layers of pain that scarred you. The things that hurt, the things people said and the bad experiences you went through. I want you to bring all of them to the front of your mind so we can "beat" their affects out of your subconscious.

When it comes to this, we have two types of thoughts we have to attack.

1. The thoughts you tie directly to an event in your life.

2. The thoughts that are connected to a pain you've hidden.

So let's deal with thoughts connected to an event first because those are the ones easiest to access.

The thoughts that usually have the biggest stronghold on us are typically connected to a past failure. We tried something, it didn't work and now every time we think about trying something else, we instantly think about the time we failed. We don't even stop to think about why we failed and correct those mistakes so we can succeed this time, we just feel like we failed then so we'll fail now.

That failure becomes a TRAP. It keeps you from moving forward. It keeps you from seeing your capabilities. It keeps you from thinking clearly about yourself. If this is you I need you to adopt this mantra.

"I FAILED & I AM A FAILURE ARE TWO DIFFERENT THINGS."

You are going to be hard pressed to find a successful person who hasn't failed before. The only difference between them and you is they took their failure as a lesson and you, like me, took it as a life sentence. Oh yeah, this was my trap. It wasn't one failure, it was MANY FAILURES that paralyzed me to the point I was suicidal. I thought to myself that I would rather be dead than to fail again. Until a friend said to me, "Look at everything you've been through. Everything you thought was a failure was actually preparation for what you're supposed to be doing."

That one sentence totally reshaped my thinking. Even though I didn't get the results I wanted from each endeavor, I did learn something different from each one. And this is the kicker. Had I succeeded on the first one, I would have never learned the lessons from the subsequent failures. Those failures put me in position to be, do and have more than I would have gotten from immediate success.

If I was successful out the gate, I would have been content with that success but failing helped me to see bigger. As I looked at what went wrong and learned how to correct it, I also learned that if I did it right the next time, it would be ten times bigger than what I was originally looking for. Failure after failure was really lesson after lesson; it all depended on my perception.

Yes, FAILURE helped me see bigger. When you look back over where you've failed before, in hindsight, can you think of different tactics you could have used to make it a bigger success than you expected? **DON'T KEEP READING STOP AND THINK ABOUT THIS FOR A SECOND**.

You are only going to be as great as the failure you went back and corrected. When we don't learn from our mistakes we relive them over and over. Eventually they become a part of us and our future decisions are based off of past mistakes. And this is how failure, TRAPS us. We get so paralyzed by what went wrong that we will sit down on our giftedness forever.

"You are only going to be as great as the failure you went back and corrected."

IS THIS YOUR TRAP?

Beating the Trap isn't just about business, it's also about becoming your best self, character wise. In my book "Boss Up: The Rules to Being a Boss" I really dug into the ten character traits you need to take full control of your life. Often times we cannot succeed professionally because of who we have become personally or we succeed professionally but our personal life is in shambles.

In either case, what needs to be changed is US. Not only can we be TRAPPED in our actions towards our goals but we can also be TRAPPED in our own bodies. We're still talking about thoughts you tie directly to an event in your life. I'm telling you now, that isn't solely about failure, that is also about traumatic events in our everyday lives.

What does this mean? It means you can have a negative experience that makes you feel you always have to respond to similar instances as if it was that same experience. What's occurring right now might not even be negative but mentally you are TRAPPED in that past experience so you tie every new experience to the old one.

Let's say you were in a relationship where your partner would stay out late and you found out they were cheating. Now you're in a new relationship and your new partner tells you they have to work late. Since you experienced getting cheated on before by someone staying out late, you instantly think your partner is cheating and you then accuse them of cheating and create a friction in your relationship. This partner could be 100% faithful to you but since you're TRAPPED from the pain of the last relationship, you mess up the new one.

This may not be what you've been through but what bad experiences have you been through in life?

What has hurt you so bad that you said to yourself "I will never let this happen again?" Now let me make this CLEAR. I am not in any way trying to get you to a place where you ignore red flags. That isn't my goal. I'm trying to get you to see how these experiences may have changed YOU.

When we experience pain we typically create defensive mechanisms to prevent us from experiencing that same pain again. What becomes problematic is when the mechanism isn't something we use it's who we become. You never want to be shaped by trauma. You can learn from it and grow through it but never let it change who you are as an individual.

Personally, I am a very supportive person. I see people doing dope things and I reach out to see how I can help. Although I have helped MANY people in their endeavors, I rarely had people to help me in mine. Slowly I began to stop randomly helping people because I was hurt by the lack of help I received. You may say "it's nothing wrong with not helping people who don't help you" and on the surface that could be true BUT being supportive was who I am and no matter what, I can't let other people's actions, dictate my character.

My work centers around helping people identify what's holding them back in order to conquer it and become their best selves, so I am big on introspection. I was able to catch myself before being non supportive became a full part of my character but many of you aren't in this line of work, so it isn't as easy for you to catch. Hell I do the work and my bad experiences still almost got to me. I believe everyone has had a bad experience that has altered who they were a little.

Can you identify yours?

You can either stop and do it now or wait until you've finished the chapter but I need you to dig deep and recall the 5 most painful experiences you've had. Once you've named them, I want you to really sit and think about how you responded to them and how you tried to protect yourself from them. The reason I want you to do this is because I want you to determine if you protected yourself by changing yourself and ended up being TRAPPED in that experience.

After doing this work, if you identified the experience(s) that your paralyzing thoughts were tied to, you have found your TRAP and now it's time to do the work to beat it. Even though you may have found a TRAP with this, as humans we are very complex. There could be more that you need to uncover, so I suggest you continue reading.

The next type of thoughts we need find are those that are connected to a pain we've hidden. These are a little harder to identify because there is no event you can tie them to. They are normally shaped by the environment you grew up in or the circumstances you live with and they shape your thinking through your subconscious. To identify this type of TRAP, you must survey your entire life to see what subliminally taught you what you can't or won't be.

Let me ask a few questions to get your mind moving in the right direction.

- When you look around your neighborhood, what does the environment inspire you to do?
- How many people do you know who are living their dream?
- How many people do you know who make over 100k a year?
- Do you think you can afford to spend a few days a week pursuing your dream?
- Are there any programs in your neighborhood that will help you get closer to your dream?
- Is there someone in your neighborhood who is already doing what you dream of?
- Can you afford post secondary education?
- What did your k-12 education equip you to do?
- Did you have to take on an adult role before you were 18?
- Is becoming your best self a common idea in your community?

The reason I ask you these questions is because I want you to find the parts of your life that drain the greatness from you. If we are to be great, everything around us needs to inspire us and whatever isn't inspiring us is planting a negative thought in our subconscious. So if you are not intentional about protecting yourself from these messages, it will be easy to fall victim to them and become TRAPPED by them.

Now I'm not saying that the messages will say "YOU CAN'T BE GREAT." That's not it at all. Your life will simply show you mediocrity or below as normal to the point where you begin to believe that this is all that life offers. You then quench the greatness that should make you stand out and fit yourself into your environment.

All of this is done subconsciously. These are thoughts that are in the back of your mind but they control how you feel about what you're capable of.

And since they're not at the forefront of your mind, it's easy for them to govern your actions and get you to feel you can't do what all the evidence says you can but TODAY we're going to start digging those thoughts out and get rid of them.

Identifying this TRAP is going to take you really looking into every area of your life. This may take a day, a week, a month even. It's not an easy task to discover these subconscious thoughts but remember the rule of thumb "if it's not inspiring you, it's planting a negative thought."

Think about every place you've spent time at. Did those places inspire you? Think about how you grew up. Did your upbringing inspire you? What do you see daily that inspires you? If you don't have inspiration all around you every day then you are being subconsciously TRAPPED.

I know reading me say "having inspiration around you all day every day" may trigger you and you think, "that's impossible." That's just those negative thoughts that were planted in your mind speaking, trying to keep you TRAPPED. Understand, it's not about having 24/7 inspiration, it's about being conscious 24/7 of when you're not being inspired.

For instance, movies have the ability to plant all types of ideas in your mind if you watch them with your mind turned off. I'm the type who looks for the messages because I do not believe entertainment is "just entertainment." So since I'm aware when watching movies, they can never plant anything in my mind.

What I'm trying to get you to see, is like movies, your environment has the ability to plant messages in your mind and if you aren't aware, you can't block them. You've been told things your whole life without you even knowing. If you feel TRAPPED, if you feel incompetent, if you feel you can't, if you feel there are no opportunities for you, that is because that's what the messages have told you all these years but guess what?

THEY'RE WRONG!

Have these types of thoughts haunted you and kept you from moving? If not these thoughts, what are some of the thoughts you've had that paralyzed you? If someone has flat out told you that you were nothing, that's different. That's an event you can tie your trauma to. I want you to think of every negative thought you think about yourself and your capabilities that no one audibly told you. Those are the thoughts we want to deal with here.

Each of those thoughts were planted in your mind by your environment or circumstances you've dealt with. It wasn't people that told you, you can't; in your perception, life was telling you, you can't. The social cues of life all around you told you that people like you, who come from where and what you come from, will never make it anywhere.

That perception has you TRAPPED. Utilize the checklist on the next page to actually do the work to fully identify your TRAP and after that, the next four chapters will give you everything you need to accomplish the goal of beating your TRAP.

STOP! Make sure you go through the checklist before proceeding.

Checklist

- ☐ Revisit every time you failed and identify a lesson you could take from each one.
- ☐ Identify what caused you to fail and what you could have done to succeed.
- ☐ Write down the 5 most painful experiences you've had and how you decided to protect yourself from it happening again.
- ☐ Assess if your protection changed your character.
- ☐ Write down the things you want to accomplish but feel like you can't.
- ☐ Write down 5 negative thoughts that keep you from taking action.

☐ Write down how your environment or life circumstances could have affirmed these thoughts.

You have now identified your TRAP.

Now let's BEAT IT!

Step 2
Becoming aware that there's more

To those of us who are physically healthy, sometimes we take the growth process of our bodies for granted. It's easy for us to think that getting taller, gaining weight and growing into a mature body is inevitable. There were even summer breaks where we came back to school and someone was three or four inches taller than the last school year. This is a common occurrence, so it appears that all we have to do in order to grow to the size that we were created to grow is continue living. However that is not true.

When we were young and our parents told us that eating our vegetables would make us strong and would help us grow, they weren't just saying that to get us to eat the things we didn't like. The truth is the body needs certain vitamins, proteins, fats, carbohydrates, etc. in order for it to be healthy. If your body isn't getting what it needs it will not grow properly. If you've ever seen a sad case of child abuse where there is a malnourished child, you can see a 16 year old with the body of an 8 year old all because they didn't get what they needed in them.

So what does all of this have to do with the transformation of our lives and Beating our TRAP? EVERYTHING! In order for us to transform our lives, we can't have the mindset a child has towards vegetables in which we look directly at what we need, have it sitting right in front of our face and say, "I don't want this." We understand that the reason some of us didn't want to eat them was because they didn't have the best taste, they weren't appealing to look at, we didn't like the smell, we didn't like the texture of it in our mouths or whatever your reason might have been. The thing is we judged them without thinking about their value; all we saw were the parts that weren't attractive to us.

This is in similitude to what a lot of us do when it comes to changing and bettering our lives. We look at the steps it takes in attaining the life we want and avoid those that don't appeal to our senses. If they don't look, feel or sound enjoyable, we attempt to skip over them, not realizing the value of each one. If we want to reach our maximum potential we cannot skip steps. You could possibly appear successful after skipping some of life's lessons but I promise you, every time you skip one you lower your potential.

If you're reading this, I'm assuming you want to drastically transform your life and Beat your TRAP. The first thing you have to understand when you're embarking on this transformational journey is that it is a process. You will not find a book, conference or lecture in this world that you can read or attend one day and see your life transformed tomorrow.

Even as I write this book I have not yet been transformed into all that I can and will be. I am nowhere near where I was but I'm just as far from who

I will be. The process of mental and intellectual growth is one we should be in until we leave this Earth and the reason being is the second phase of Beating your TRAP.

The second phase of this journey is simply becoming aware that there is more. Throughout this book when I speak of "More" what I am speaking of is the potential in the world or in yourself that you were previously blind to. Your "More" is something you've always been capable of but had not discovered yet. It is that idea, that dream, that job, that character and ultimately the life that was laying dormant, waiting for you to realize the possibility that you could live it. This is your "More."

This phase is a two thought phase. First you have to become aware that there is more to life and second that there is more to you. Without the driving force behind this phase we are TRAPPED in the life we're living today. Of course there are exceptions; a person could hit the lottery and change their life but to the rest of us who aren't fortunate enough to hit for mega millions, we are bound to our circumstances if we aren't cognizant of more.

(You cannot achieve that which you do not know exists. In order to grow you must see that there is something for you to grow into. Many of us never reach the heights in life we could because we don't push life to its limits. In fact, we put limits on our lives.

We stay where we're comfortable, where everyone we know has always been and we settle for what's at our eyes level. We never seek those things that are out of our sight; those things are the "More" we're capable of but rarely tap into.)

      These two thoughts have to be working simultaneously in order to move forward. I believe most people have one of these and are lacking the other, thus hindering their advancement. If you believe you have more to offer the world but your world view doesn't offer you the opportunity to showcase it, you will bury your gifts. Likewise, if you see that the world offers more but don't think that you have anything inside of you of any value, you will never grow into being fully productive In society.

That is why both of these thoughts have to work together. Once you see more in the world and more in yourself, you can then begin working to attain them. In other cases, some individuals are surrounded with so much poverty and pessimism that they don't have either. Their view of the world is limited and their view of themselves is even lower but no matter where you fall I can help you get up. Let's delve into how the three possibilities look so we can find what we're missing and awaken ourselves.

It all starts with you being honest with YOU! You're reading this alone and no one knows your thoughts, so think for a few moments on these two questions.

- **Do I believe that there is more to life than the life I see every day?**
- **Do I believe that there is more to me than who I am right now?**

Some people believe that there is more to life but do not agree that there's more to themselves. How does this look? Are you someone that is able to see how others are making moves and are experiencing drastic change in their lives but you can't see yourself doing the same? Do you see how people are marketing their talents, creating apps or re-inventing themselves for the better but think that you don't have anything like that to offer?

You fall in the category of those that need to be aware that it is more within them.

You already know what's possible and how far there is to go in life, you just need to be able to see yourself as someone that can go that far. You question your talents, your capability and if someone like you could ever do something like what you see. This is a matter of learning how to identify aspects of yourself that you didn't know existed. As we go further into this chapter I will help you to do so.

There are others who believe there is more to them but don't believe the world has more to offer them. How does this look? If you find yourself with new ideas that no one else has had and feel like you aren't embraced by others and there is no room for your ideas or personality in this world, you fall into the category that need to be aware that there is more to the world.

The world is constantly evolving and there is something new every day. Thinking that there is no place for you shows that you haven't exposed yourself to everything that is out there. No matter how peculiar you may be, there is a group of people that are either like you or will accept you. If you desire to do a thing that no one else is doing, that doesn't mean you can't do it because it hasn't been done, it means you have to be the first. Our world has always been fixated on what's new. When you feel that whatever inside of you can't fit in the world as you know it, it's time to expand the world you know. Let me help you do so.

If you don't fit into either of these, DO NOT FEEL LIKE YOU ARE A LOST CAUSE! You are not the only one and this is not an indictment of your character; this only enlightens you to the fact that you haven't been exposed to enough. Due to your upbringing, your environment and the teachings of those older than you, you were limited in what you could believe because you had limited information. It's not your fault that you were never informed. It will however be your fault if now you choose to stay uninformed.

What I am about to say is going to be completely ignorant in the purest form of the word but I need you to understand how your views are limited by what you haven't been taught.

When I was 9 years old my family moved to a very diverse neighborhood that had a very strong Asian presence. My first week there at the playground I came across something I never knew existed: Cambodians. I greeted a young Asian boy and thought that he was Chinese but he informed me that he was Cambodian.

My siblings and I were blown away because we ignorantly thought that all Asians were Chinese. I don't know if it was because we didn't get to that part of Asia in school yet or because we only saw Chinese movies and Chinese stores, whatever the variables were, we had no knowledge of Cambodia and the people who were from there.

This was not something that anyone could fault me for. My life's experience never afforded me the opportunity to know about this nationality but once it did it was now my job to make sure I was informed on this subject. So after the interaction with this boy I began to ask all the children I met one question, "Where are you from?" This neighborhood was so diverse I ended up with not only Cambodian friends but I had friends that were Portuguese, Vietnamese and Philipino. I had now made myself more aware of races I previously had no knowledge of and made it a point to continue to keep myself aware.

The first thing that we have to do if we want to Beat our TRAP and transform our lives is put ourselves in positions to be aware of more than what we presently are informed of now. The same way I asked every child where they were from, we have to ask questions according to everything we see. Ninety nine plus percent of the world are not privy to the top of any chain, so regardless of whatever is in our views, we need to be educating ourselves on what is governing what we see.

If we go to a bank we know the teller is not at the top of the banking world. The teller has a manager that oversees the bank; however the manager still isn't at the top. The highest place on the chain we can see at the bank is the manager but just because that's all we see doesn't mean that's the highest position you can be within the company.

What plagues most people is that we settle for what we can see and never investigate the things that are unseen. If you become a bank manager and never look at job postings that are above your pay grade then you will stay at your pay grade. But if you make yourself aware of the positions that are higher than yours, you now have the option of pursuing them.

I am not implying that you cannot be satisfied with being a bank manager but in whatever you're doing, put yourself in a position to have options. You will never know the different things you might like to do if you are ignorant of their existence. Search out the highest peak in everything you do in order to find what spot on the ladder is the place for you. Don't be the person who settled because you didn't know that there were more options.

Now, you might not be in banking but whatever field you're in or aspire to be in, I want you to **think of the highest position you've physically seen so far. Now, I want you to find what's next up.** Don't settle for what you see or what you've been told; make it your business to search for the top. Once you begin to find what else is out there then you'll be able to find where you can fit in. This is not about reaching the top since mathematically everyone can't be at the top; this is about broadening your scope of possibilities in order to find whatever your niche is.

"So many people are TRAPPED where they are and have never found their purpose; not because they weren't capable of doing so but because they never knew the thing they were purposed to do existed."

Whenever we hear the phrase "I never would have imagined I'd be here." What the person is saying is there was no way that they could have thought of living how they're living or doing what they're doing on their own. The only way they were able to attain something they couldn't dream up was by being informed about it somehow.

One of my favorite movies is The Social Network. It shows how Mark Zuckerberg created and successfully launched The Facebook. This social media site went on to make billions but until Mark met Sean Parker he couldn't see his creation as such a world changing entity. Once he was aware of what he could do with his invention, he took it to unprecedented heights.

- **Question is, what is it that you're capable of but can't see the possibility?**
- **What gifts do you have in which you don't even see that there is a market for?**
- **What position in your company would you be perfect in if you knew there was such a thing?**
- **What would you do if you found a list of everything that possibly could be done?**

Your transformation will not begin until you find answers to questions like these. Until you begin to fill in the unknown, you will be restricted from being any more than you know right now. Don't miss out on going higher because you didn't know there was a higher. Question everything, learn as much as you can and never stop thinking about more. Not to be gluttonous but to make sure you're maximizing your existence.

Write down everything you're capable of and every talent you have **(literally write them down)** then grab a hold of this one fact. There is a market for EVERYTHING!! Whatever you're good at can be turned into a business. There are things that we could do but don't, simply because we don't know it can be done. That is what will make you an innovator. The first to do something is always stepping out on something that appears strange in the beginning until people realize how much they need what that person offers.

There is more to what you can do in life. Take some time to make yourself aware of what your MORE is.

Character Transformation

Now, we've been dealing with finances but I know some of you want to transform your character and this is where the second thought in this phase comes in. You can come from a family and neighborhood where the majority of the people are rude, obnoxious and don't have anyone's best interest in mind but themselves. Or you could be surrounded by criminals.

Whatever your character flaws are, the same principle applies. You have to seek people who you can identify with who possess the qualities you would like to see in yourself. It's very unfortunate but you can be encased by a barrage of bad traits and prohibited from seeing yourself in another light, which is why you have to be aware that there is more to you.

I don't believe anyone is a product of their environment, I believe they are products of thinking their environment defines them. Surviving in some neighborhoods is done by understanding "how things work" there. If you know what the people are like, what the people do, how the people respond and what's acceptable or unacceptable, you can make it in the worst places. The problem with this is, (as we discussed in chapter 1) after awhile, adapting to survive turns into your way of life. It's no longer a defensive mechanism, it's who you are.

Over the years, I have seen so many cases of this on social media. When a person first joins a site, they post in a manner that represents their true selves. After some time they see that certain things are heralded while others are looked down on. Often times, anything that is positive is looked down on so in order to fit in with their circle of social media friends, they post according to what's popular. After some time of posting just to fit in, it then takes over the persons thinking and they begin to identify with their social media image and not who they truly are.

Once we identify ourselves with or as something, we concede our ability to grow past it. We've all encountered or heard of someone that was doing something they knew was wrong and justified it by saying "This is just how I am." This statement is blocking the individual from change. They can't see themselves as anything other than what they've agreed to identify with, even if it's making life harder for them.

This could be you. You may have bad qualities about yourself that you blame on your family and society which the blame is probably 100% accurate. Even though they may have shaped you, the truth is you are responsible for staying that way. *You are not bound to stay how you've always been.* Contrary to popular belief, people can and do change. But in order to change, you have to see yourself in the change that you want.

Another common phrase we often utter is "I can't see myself……" As soon as we say these words we curse ourselves from becoming whatever comes after them. There was a time I couldn't see myself going to college and as long as I couldn't see it, was as long as I never attended.

Are there some great things that you just can't see yourself doing?

Are you intrigued by the life of someone else or something they're doing but as soon as you attempt to think about it being you, you can't ever see yourself in that position?

If so, it's time to change your thinking.

People aren't born great, nasty, as killers, loving, kind, hateful or any other characteristic you can have, we're born with the potential to be any which one. You can have two children raised in the same home with drug addicted parents; one gets hooked on drugs while you can't get the other to even take a Tylenol. This happens solely because of the visualization of the individuals. One couldn't see their selves ever getting high, the other could. The way they saw themselves dictated who they became.

- **How do you see yourself?**
- **Do you see yourself getting over the pain of your childhood?**
- **Do you see yourself ever being able to be faithful and loyal to someone?**
- **Do you see yourself being able to be nicer, more loving, more honest, etc.?**

There is so much more to who you are than who you've been. It's easy for us to look at how we've lived and think that changing those behaviors are next to impossible but the truth is, changing the behaviors is easy, the hard part is changing your thinking. In order to unlock your best qualities you must first realize that you already posses them. Deep down inside of you is a person who is completely the opposite of who you are now. Everything that you want to be is in you lying dormant waiting for you to become aware of its existence. Your transformation is one moment away. At the very moment you discover what you're capable of transformation will be instantaneous.

This does not mean that all of your actions and thoughts will be perfectly lined up with your new life but that your change has occurred. A big misunderstanding about change is thinking it occurs once we can see it. Even though it is evidenced once we can see it, it takes place the instant a person makes the decision to be different. The world can't visibly see it yet but on the inside change has taken place.

Will you decide right now to be different? To unlock the parts of you that are not constrained or influenced by your environment. Will you decide right now to dig deep into your being and awaken the sleeping potential for you to be your best? If you choose right now to take your eyes off the world and solely look inside yourself, you will find that you have the capacity to grow into a completely new version of you. As R Buckminster Fuller said, "There's nothing about a caterpillar that lets you know it's going to be a butterfly." I don't care how your life has looked in the past, when you are ready, like the caterpillar you too can morph into something more beautiful.

STOP! Make sure you go through the checklist before proceeding.

Checklist

- ☐ Write down your talents, skills and anything you're capable of.
- ☐ Identify your greatest potential.
- ☐ Research, until you find exactly how far the potential can take you.
- ☐ Pinpoint and write out the negative things you've identified with.
- ☐ Write out the positive counterparts and see how you identify with them.
- ☐ Create an end vision of yourself. (How you want your character, job/business and life to look.)
- ☐ Make sure every decision you make lines up with that end goal.

B. F. Nkrumah

Step 3

Recognize the changes that need to be made in you

Now that you've identified your TRAP and you're aware that there is more to life and that there is more to you, it's on to step three: recognizing the changes that need to be made in you. The question you need to ask yourself in order to assess your life is this **"Is the life I'm leading, leading me to the life I want?"** The basis of this question will be asked in four forms throughout this chapter. You've already identified the "More" that you desire and have the capability of attaining, now it's a matter of correcting the mindset, actions, surroundings and people that are hindering you from getting there.

    Albert Einstein defined insanity as doing the same things repetitively and expecting different results. This definition shows us how improbable it is to change the circumstances of one's life without first changing their decision making. Thus, we have to look at every area of our lives and determine if it is helping us move towards our goal, away from our goal or causing us to remain stagnant. Remember, if it isn't inspiring you, it's planting a negative thought.

The Lottery's slogan is "You have to play to win." If you have made up in your mind that you don't play the lottery but then see the Powerball at 400 million and you want to win it, the only way to make that possible is to change the fact that you don't play the lottery. Once you change how you think about it and then change your actions to actually play it, now you've set yourself up in a position to be able to win.

This goes for everything in life that you wish to have. You cannot receive what you would like, if you're against altering yourself. I know it just doesn't sit well with us to think that we're not perfect but the fact is we're not. This does not mean that we're incompetent and do not possess the skills needed to elevate our lives, this means that we have to constantly check to see what might not be right about us, so that we can fix it in order to keep moving towards our destination.

Years ago I was a mechanic for Philadelphia's transit company. My daily assignment was to do preventive maintenance inspections on buses. In these inspections, we would take buses that appear to be working just fine and examine them from top to bottom as a precautionary measure to see if there is anything wrong that can't be seen by plain sight. Thing is, there are things that can be wrong with a bus that doesn't immediately prevent it from driving but if it goes unchecked, sooner or later it will break down en route to the stops it's supposed to make.

We have to look at our lives like these buses and understand that we have stops that we are supposed to make. There is a greatness about you that you are supposed to live out but many of us have broken down on the way because we thought all was well since we were still moving. We still exist, we're still paying our bills, we still have some people that like us, we're still doing "OK." This is a sign of a person that is "existing" and not LIVING.

We've all been caught in periods of stagnation where we have accepted the cards we were dealt, so to speak. We looked around at our lives, we looked at our parents lives and we looked at the lives of those around us and came to the conclusion that this is just who I am. While it is true that it is who you are at the present moment, if you want to transform your life you have to ask yourself **"WHY am I this way now?"** *This is where assessing your life comes to play.*

The first thing that you have to assess is your mindset and ask yourself...

"Is the way I think leading me to the life I want?"

Chances are the answer to this question is no. During the past few years we've heard so much about the 1% of the country that makes more than the other 99% combined. I suggest to you that the majority of those in the 99% will never raise their living situations because their mindsets aren't big enough.

They won't leave a legacy because they don't think about legacies. They won't leave lasting impressions on other's lives because they don't think about building their character to one that makes people remember them after they're gone. They will never own their own business, marry the type of spouse they want, be the person they want to be, make the friends they want to make, etc. all because their thinking is wrong.

When you look at the "More" you identified in step two, **how has your thinking been the past few years in regards to you making it a reality?**

- Did you think it was possible?
- Did you have an optimistic or a pessimistic view about it?
- Did you think you had what it took to reach it or were you thinking that you didn't?

During this phase you have to search for whatever thoughts were keeping you from attempting to change.

Some people don't want to change because they're used to their way of living and are fearful of not knowing exactly how life will be. Some are afraid of failing and hearing I told you so. Some think it's too hard. Some think it's too late. Some think they're too set in their ways to ever be different. Whatever your thought process has been, you have to challenge it and find the error in your thinking.

Almost all of these negative thoughts we think have no facts in which they are based upon. As soon as you desire to do something great, one of these thoughts will come in your mind telling you that you can't achieve it but without any proof of it. There is no evidence that suggests you can't, so you have to challenge why you think the way you do.

This might sound crazy but sometimes you have to argue with yourself. When your sub-conscious tells you, you can't, you have to refute it with evidence that shows you can. Don't trust your own thinking, only trust facts. When your thinking speaks against your goal, you can persuade yourself with evidence and begin to change your thinking.

Our actions are a direct result of our thinking, so any change in our thoughts will alter the course of our life. It is up to us to alter the negative and impeding thoughts and replace them with positive and advancing ones. You can't Beat your TRAP without first transforming your mind. If there is a better life that you want and it's a priority to you, you have to examine yourself and recognize every thought that has to be changed.

You have to question the why behind everything you habitually do. Every conclusion you've come to about your present self that doesn't help you better your future self has to be contested. Any thought that forces you to settle for less than the best version of you has to be replaced.

Take some time and think about your world views. Think about how you've felt concerning who controls the parameters of your life. Think about why you believe that you can't do something. Now this is not something that you may be able to do right away but over the next couple weeks, every time you notice you have a negative view of yourself or your capabilities recognize it as a way of thinking that needs to be changed.

I taught a class once on "speaking like God" in which we had to understand how we have the power to speak authoritatively into our lives, whether the things we spoke were helping or hurting us. After the class, my students and I would consciously catch ourselves before we spoke something negative into our lives and if we heard someone say something negative we would quickly point it out and have them correct it. Point being, once we received the information, we had to make an effort to catch every harmful word.

You have now received this information about your thoughts. Now you have to make the effort all day everyday to catch every harmful thought. You have to place new thoughts in your mind that will replace your pessimistic subconscious thoughts. You have to rid your mind of everything that makes you think you can't. *Once you change your mind your actions will soon follow.*

Question 2.

"Are my current actions leading me to the life I want?"

As I just stated, once you change your mind your actions are soon to follow but some things are so customary that you do them without thinking. So even if your thoughts are different, you still need to purposely check the things you do. They say that after 21 days of repetitively doing something, it turns into a habit. This can be something negative that you unknowingly fell into or something positive you intentionally put yourself in place to do. Whether positive or negative we all have actions that are routine. This section is about finding the actions that are not leading us in the right direction.

Your "More" might have been a higher position at your job, starting an innovative business or drastically changing your character whether being more honorable, friendly, honest, courteous etc.

Whatever your "More" is, there are actions that need to take place to get to it and ones that are keeping you from it. The simplest way to identify these bad actions is to find out what steps are necessary to reaching your goal, write them down and make an attempt to stop doing everything that isn't on your to-do list.

Let's say you do want that higher position at your job. You know to qualify for it you have to be knowledgeable of the required duties, you have to be trustworthy, have a good rapport and a great work ethic. There are actions that have to take place in order to posses these qualities and there are actions that will show that you don't possess them.

If you need to be knowledgeable of the higher position, you can't be the person in the workplace that won't do anything extra because it's outside of your job description. The habit of coming in and making sure you only do the minimum required to keep your employment status has to change. Likewise, if they are looking for you to be trustworthy, that habit of coming in late has to change. How can they trust you with more responsibility if they're not sure if you'll be at work or not?

Some of you might just want to change certain parts of your character. If you want a particular characteristic to become a part of who you are, force yourself to do it for twenty one days. There was a time I thought suits and shoes were uncomfortable and I would I rush to take them off after I was obligated to wear them. Then I started a job where I had to wear one to work Monday through Friday and I had to wear one Sundays at church. Six days a week I forced myself to wear these uncomfortable suits and shoes because I had to. After a while I realized I wasn't rushing to take them off anymore; *what was uncomfortable became comfortable after some time.*

As you are working towards beating your TRAP, there are going to be some uncomfortable times. There are thing you've grown accustomed to doing that you need to stop and when you first attempt to, it isn't going to be easy. But let me ask you this, are you comfortable being TRAPPED? If you're reading this you're obviously trying to escape, so you have to make a choice. Be uncomfortable in life overall and keep a comfortable action or cut the action out and be uncomfortable for a time but headed towards a comfortable life. YOU CHOOSE!

Let's say you want to be a nicer person but you're use to being mean, it will be uncomfortable for you to be nice to certain people at first but after forcing yourself, it will become second nature. If you want to raise your level of integrity you have to stop having "more than one face". You have to force yourself to be who you say you are at all times and no longer switch up depending on the circumstance and who's around. Whatever quality you want has an opposite action that you must get rid of. So, for every trait that you want you must first ask yourself "Am I the opposite?"

You can't beat your TRAP if you're unwilling to identify and make the necessary changes. Often times we want everything in our lives to change EXCEPT US and it doesn't work that way. The only thing in our lives that we can fully control is ourselves, so our person is the first thing we need to be looking to change when we're aspiring to get more out of life. Remember this, in life you attract that which you are not what you want.

Being honest with yourself is a must if you want to beat your TRAP. You have to come down off your high horse and admit that you aren't as great of a person you thought you were but know that once you find out what your flaws are, you can be that great individual. **Now is the time to look at how you behave in every area of your life. How do you act when you're with certain people, on the job, in public, in your neighborhood and most importantly when you're all alone? What are some of the things you do that you know aren't helping you go forward?**

I can't name every possible action that every person could be doing but you know what your personal issue is. You have to take a good look at what it takes to get where you want and determine if your current actions will lead you there. If not, they are the changes you need to make if you intend on transforming your life. In order to get the answers on how to make your future brighter you have to question your present. *Questioning your present and past actions will show you how to transform your future.*

Question 3

"Are my surroundings leading me to the life I want?"

I know you might not have a choice in where you were raised and might not have a choice in where you can or cannot live; what you do have however is the option to choose what type of environments you put yourself in a position to be influenced by. This is not about being able to afford living in upscale neighborhoods or being a part of elite private clubs, this is about removing yourself from places infected with despair. It's about being in places where hope is visible. No matter how bad your neighborhood is, there are places you can go that will inspire you to achieve more. And remember AGAIN, *if it is not inspiring you, it's planting negative seeds.*

Before we talk about these places, we have to deal with your current surroundings. **Where do you spend most of your time?** Where you spend the most of your time literally shows where you are in life and it also shows what possibilities you have for your future, whether good or bad. We are all shaped by what we receive in life. This does not mean that one cannot overcome the environment they were raised in but in order to do so, they have to mentally detach themselves from their surroundings.

You may see a child that grew up in a very impoverished, violent and ignorant neighborhood, become a neurosurgeon. If you saw that then you also saw them surrounding themselves with books. They were in school early and stayed late. They were in science clubs, science competitions, at science fairs and everywhere they could get that had to do with science. If you see a child involved in all of these aforementioned things, a person's first thought about them would be that one day this child is going to do something that has to do with science. Why? *Because the atmospheres in which you take in the most information dictate where you go in life.*

So I ask again, **where do you spend the most of your time?** For example, if you spend most of your time in a bar, you are taking in alcohol that will lead you to being drunk. You are taking in information on liquor and from people who are intoxicated also that will lead you to God knows where. Being there daily gives you a high probability of being a future alcoholic or an individual that makes choices based off of drunken information, simply because that is what you are taking in.

Our lives are the sum total of what we've learned. Some of us were in places where we learned right from wrong, proper etiquette, that we have the ability to attain our dreams and how to attain them. Normally these type of people end up obtaining their dreams. On the other hand, some are raised in places where they learn it's an honor to blow yourself up and kill people of other races. Normally these type of people end up dead. The only real difference between the successful individual and the suicide bomber is the information they took in from where they were.

The leaders of these extremist groups normally take young boys, remove them from their homes and surround them with their teaching to get them to do what they want them to do. There have been cases where young boys didn't want to be suicide bombers so they ran away from the compound. They knew that if they stayed, death was inevitable, so the only way to ensure that they wouldn't end up a victim of their surroundings was to get away from it.

When you allow yourself to stay surrounded by environments that do not help you grow, you are committing suicide. You are killing every chance you have at beating your TRAP because guess what, you are choosing to stay where the TRAP is. We've been trained to have this undying loyalty to the area we were raised in but where is your loyalty to your future success?

You are not obligated to stay in places that don't help you grow. Don't let anyone guilt you into staying in a TRAP by saying "You're changing." Changing for the better is what life is all about. You will never get to where you want to be in life by staying in the same places you've always been at. All you will do is blow up your chances of getting your "More."

Although a suicide bomber example may be extreme, I think by now you get where I'm going.

So what places do you need to run away from?
If you stay where you are, you are bound to be a victim of what you're learning there.

Do the places you frequent give you any information that will get you closer to your goal? If not, you need to change your surroundings. You cannot continue to be in places that don't have the aptitude to help you advance.

Over the next few weeks document ALL of your time. Look over where you spent the most time and assess if you are receiving any valuable information there. If not then run away like the boys that didn't want to become suicide bombers. Find a place that will teach you what you need in order to reach your "More."

Question 4

"Are the people I'm around leading me to the life I want?"

When I was younger one of my older cousins was having a talk with me on how to be successful and said something to me that I will never forget. He said "Only hang with people that have what you want or want what you want." His motive in this conversation was to get me away from certain people I was hanging with that he knew would drag me down. He made me understand the importance of being around like minded people.

Jim Rohn said "You are the average of the five people you spend the most time with." If you are around people with aspirations, that are driven, that are educated, that genuinely care for the welfare of those around them or anything of this sort, then you fall right in the middle of those things. However, if you are around people that are backbiters, ignorant, have no ambition, just want to sit around and do nothing all day or anything of this sort, then you fall right in the middle of those things. So ask yourself, **who are the top five people I spend the most time with and what do they do or aspire to do?**

Not only are we influenced by our surroundings we are more so influenced by who we join ourselves with. The bible asks this question, "Can two walk together, except they agree?" I know we don't like to be categorized by other people but can you really hang with someone daily and not agree with how they live? The more you're around someone the more your beliefs will become one in the same or the only reason you're around them in the first place is because you are alike in some areas.

The normal course of creating friendships is more times than not based upon what you have in common. As we grow and mature, we naturally distance ourselves from certain friends, not because we lose love for them but because we no longer have anything in common. If you're going to grow to live the life you desire, you're going to have to distance yourself from everyone that doesn't want the type of life that you want. This does not mean that you completely severe the relationship, look down on them or dislike them, you just can't hang around them in the same capacity as you did before.

As a man who has transformed from a drug dealer to a preacher, 7 time author, mentor and internationally respected thought leader, there are people I still love dearly to this date that I can't hang around every day. I do not love them any less than I did when we spent all day together, I simply understand that if I'm going to reach my "More" it's imperative that I spend the majority of my time with individuals that will help or inspire me to reach it.

Almost all of my friends have been my friends since I was under ten, so trust me I know this is hard to do but your future depends on it. You have to remove the people from your daily circle that don't have qualities you want figured into your average. This may be the one thing you don't have to wait a few weeks to identify; we all know what friends we have that aren't concerned about advancing in life. You have to make a choice. *Continue hanging around the same people and living the same life you're living now or change your friends and change your life. Choose carefully.*

Remember the question. **Is the life I'm leading, leading me to the life I want?** Let this question be a measuring stick for every decision you make. Before you think, act, congregate or associate make sure whatever it is, is helping you to become better. Anything that doesn't measure up needs to be recognized as something you need to change. Make those changes and you're halfway to transformation.

STOP! Make sure you go through the checklist before proceeding.

Checklist

- ☐ Identify the thoughts that aren't leading you to your "More" when you have them.
- ☐ Find facts that disprove these thoughts.
- ☐ Figure out why you have believed these thoughts in the past.
- ☐ When you catch yourself having a negative thought stop and replace it with a positive one.
- ☐ Find out what steps you need to take to reach your "More."
- ☐ Write down your actions that aren't leading you towards it.
- ☐ Force yourself to do the things you need to do for 21 days.

- ☐ Write down the top 5 places you spend the most time at.
- ☐ Asses if those places are leading to your goal.
- ☐ Locate places you can spend time at that will help you get to your goal.
- ☐ Write down the top 5 people you spend the most time with.
- ☐ Write down what they aspire to do. (If nothing or something negative remove them from your top 5)
- ☐ Find some friends that desire to live the type of life you want.

Step 4
Preparing when it's not your time

When I talk about "Your time" I'm talking about the period when all the stars are aligned for you. When opportunities are present and you are 100% ready to seize them. You have all the information you need, you have had all the practice that is necessary to be confident, you're completely capable of tackling what you could not before and you have waited without attempting to force it. This period is your time. It is a time where no one can stop, slow down or hinder you. Unfortunately many of us attempt to live in this period before it's actually our time.

We decide to move before we have adequate knowledge, before we've practiced enough to get it down pact, before we possess all the skills we need and definitely haven't waited until the opportunity was present. This is what I want to help you avoid. Since transformation is a process, you can't put yourself in certain areas without it being complete. You have to go through your entire preparation period before you can approach an opportunity.

There are three words that you have to acclimate yourself with during this phase, "I'm not ready." We've all seen college athletes that decided to stay in college another year instead of being drafted to the pros, a person opt out of talking to someone that hurt them or a person that postponed the launch of something and these three words were the reason why.

The college kid knew they needed to work on something that would get exposed at the professional level. The hurt individual knew they couldn't face the person without either being hurt more or attempting to hurt the other person. The person who postponed their launch knew there were vital things they were missing that would decrease the effectiveness of their launch. In every case similar to this, the people knew they weren't ready and were willing to wait until they had everything they needed before they moved on.

It is easy for some to have this outlook while others struggle with the concept of waiting and/or thinking they don't have what it takes at the present moment. This is going to sound really simple but the reason this phase is so important is because before you have fully transformed, you have not fully transformed. You can't apply for a job that requires a bachelor's degree before you finish high school. You can't visit someone that is having a tough time if you know you're still insensitive. At some points in our lives we're just not ready. This is not a knock on who we're becoming it's just a fact that we're not there yet.

While I do not believe that any part of the transformation process is more important than the other, this phase is where most people give up. We have been conditioned to expect everything to be fast and get even faster. Cellular companies are marketing how fast their phones internet is and have us all upgrading from the 3g to the 4g to the 5glte and if we be honest, we have no idea what any of it is. All we know is that they say it's faster. So if it's faster we have to have it because we want everything NOW.

This thinking really hinders us while we're in the process of transforming because transformation is not something that happens overnight. Even if you decide to be different and have committed to a new lifestyle, it still takes time to completely break habits. So in the time between you deciding to change and actually seeing the maximum results of your decision, you have to prepare yourself for the day that you reach that point.

If a person isn't very well spoken, doesn't have a broad vocabulary and is accustomed to using urban vernacular, they cannot expect to change today and speak in boardroom tomorrow. They have to spend countless hours reading in order to learn words that are suitable for the arenas they desire to speak in. They also have to spend time learning to speak and pronunciate words in a manner that is fitting for the hearers. This is something that can take years for some. Only those who are fully committed to the end result will achieve it; others will quit because they feel as if they should be at a certain place at a particular time and they're just not there yet.

Fact of the matter is, there is an allotted time for everything to happen in our lives and there is nothing you can do to speed up the process. I've come to realize that attempting to speed things up actually slows them down. We cannot spend more time trying to create opportunities than we spend preparing to be equipped to take advantage of one. Our primary purpose is to work on our gifts and perfect them to the point that others are forced to recognize them. Taking time away from making yourself better adds time on to when you'll be ready for the life you want.

Every moment you spend trying to speed up your time is a precious moment you lose from preparation. We can easily turn a one year process into a ten year process all because we were focused on being something and not becoming something. In our adult age we are similar to children on a road trip continually asking are we there yet. We can't sit, wait and let the natural process take its course; we have to be fixated on where we want to be and being there now. Not understanding that stepping out too early will only cause discouragement and/or embarrassment.

If you are working on your anger, after a week you should not intentionally put yourself in a room with the one person you know pushes all of your buttons. You're not ready for them yet. All that will come out of the interaction is you expressing your frustrations and in turn feeling as if you will never be able to control your anger. That thought could potentially cause you to give up on your quest for changing simply because you stepped out too soon. This does not show that you will never conquer your emotion it just shows that it wasn't time for you to attempt that yet.

On the other side of the coin, if you desire to be a singer and you're working with a vocal coach that believes with more training, you can be a star but you're ready to be a star right now and you audition for American Idol and end up being laughed at by the entire country, that will leave you feeling the worst embarrassment you ever felt. This does not mean you don't have ability but since you tried to speed up the course, you ended up embarrassed when all you had to do was keep preparing.

These two things may not be what you're trying to transform into but they speak to those wanting to change character issues and those chasing their dreams. The point of it is, whatever your "More" is, there is going to be a process that needs to run its full course before you are able to completely live it out.

You don't want to come out half way through your development and hit a wall in life because you're not equipped. It's just a guess but I don't think a caterpillar that comes out the cocoon too early will have an appearance that is pleasing on the eye. That's why they stay the full course, so when they come out they're fully butterflies and not an in between version of one.

Wait your time so that you're not living as an unfinished version of yourself, opening the door for disappointment. Your time will come but only when it's right. Until then continue to work on you. Work on seeing more to the world and yourself. Work on changing your mind, actions, surroundings and association. Work on your character flaws. Attain more knowledge on your field of interest. Don't let a day go by without you doing something that will make you better. **Opportunities will come, but the question is, will you be ready?**

Another thing that causes people to give up during this stage is feeling hypocritical. You're saying that you're changing but at the moment your life still looks how it did before you made the decision, so you give up because it doesn't appear to be working. I'll state it again and again. Transformation is a process and can be a lengthy one. It's also a case by case basis; you cannot look at someone else and think "Why did they change so fast and I'm still struggling?" *Your process is your process.* There is no race nor is there a prize for who transforms the fastest. Your attention has to be on becoming a better you day after day.

You can't look at your day one or even your day forty and measure it to your expected end; when things don't appear to be changing, just keep trying. I'll tell a little of my story. For years of my life, I was engulfed in the streets. Selling drugs was how I financed my life and carrying a gun was how I protected myself. On the day I decided to change and start attending church, the only thing that changed in my life was I started attending church. Sunday after

Sunday I would go to church with my gun then leave church and sell drugs. What else was I going to do?

I still needed to eat and pay bills so I couldn't instantaneously give up selling drugs, I wouldn't have survived. I couldn't walk around without a gun because I still had enemies who hadn't decided to change their lives so I had to protect myself. Even though I made a conscious decision to change and committed myself to changing, my appearance to the world was still that of a drug dealer.

The more I continued going to church the more I was convicted about my lifestyle and **SLOWLY** (key word), the things I was previously doing, I began to stop. In my opinion, it was impossible for me to join church one day and give up my entire street life the next. I had to gradually transform into the man writing this book today.

While there are people that believe you can quit things cold turkey, I am not one of them. I never suggest to anyone I counsel to shock their life, attempting to do a 180 degree turn around in 24 hours. What I tell everyone is set out to be better today than you were yesterday. That's all I can expect people to do. One key principle in *transformation we need to grab a hold of is that transformation is not hinged on cutting things out of our lives; it is rooted in adding to it.*

Notice how my transformation began. I added going to church to a lifestyle that was void of church. Every minute that I spent at a church activity was a minute I wasn't spending doing something wrong. By default I wasn't doing some of the things I use to do simply because I was busy doing something else. This is how you prepare when it's not your time.

In 2006, I couldn't focus on being an author of seven books, a public speaker and a transformation coach in 2020, I had to make 2006 Bamidele a better Bamidele each day and that's how I ended up where I am today. If you've went through the first three steps of Beating Your Trap and you find yourself here like I was, keep working on you. If you have an end goal in mind but your present doesn't look anything like it, keep working on you. Even if you don't appear to others to have made the slightest change, still continue working on you.

You will make it to your goal if you continue to prepare for it. Right now it's not time for you to be over your hurts yet. It's not time for your character to be 100% whole. It may not be time for you to get that promotion or start that business but it is always time to prepare yourself for the opportunity to do so. *Your "More" is just a process away.* Keep getting better, keep learning, keep assessing you and never stop growing. Even when it feels like your growth is stagnant, understand that not going backwards is still growth.

It is imperative that we learn to handle life when it's not our time to bloom. How you conduct yourself in these times will determine the magnitude of what you can do when it is. Training is a vital part of success in any field. The more you train the more likely you will be able to seize your moment when it comes. The first two phases will mean nothing to your transformation if you don't make the proper preparations to move to your final phase.

- **Do you have anything planned that will help you get ready for an opportunity if it presents itself?**
- **Are you doing anything daily that will make you better than you were yesterday?**
- **Are you doing everything you can to make yourself knowledgeable and equipped?**

Whatever it is that you want, create a practice drill for it. Sometimes you might have to get dressed, look in the mirror and act and talk out how you want to present yourself. In schools and jobs they have fire drills to teach you how you should respond in the advent of fire. I ask you, how would you be able to respond if an opportunity fell in your lap?

We see people go viral all the time and a week later they're trying to capitalize off of it but by then their moment has passed. If only they were prepared and had products ready for the moment those millions of people had their eyes on them they could have gotten rich. But since they didn't prepare, all they got was 15 seconds of fame. Don't let this be you.

Shift your focus from opportunity to preparation. There will always be opportunities whether big or small but will you be able to take advantage of them is the question. Don't blow a viral moment by trying to go viral and not preparing to capitalize off of it.

Now I cannot list every type of preparation or everything one might desire to transform into but the principles are all the same. If you know what and how you want to be, you have to put forth the effort to find out what it takes to get there and do everything from A-Z before you try to take advantage of an opportunity. Even if one presents itself you have to turn it down if you're not ready for it and dedicate yourself to being ready the next time.

In track and field the runners get to their mark then they get set and they have to wait for their go. The go is completely out of their hands but getting to the mark and getting set is fully in their control. This phase is all about you getting to your mark and getting set to go. It's about you doing all the necessary training possible so that you can even qualify to be in the race. (Not that you're competing with anyone other than yourself.) Once you've trained, got to your mark and are set, now you just have to wait for the go. Don't try to take off too early because you will be disqualified. All you have to do is get ready. Right now get the opportunity out of your mind and focus on being ready for it when it comes.

STOP! Make sure you go through the checklist before proceeding.

Checklist

- ☐ Identify what you spend time doing daily and cut out everything that isn't helping you grow.
- ☐ **Spend one hour each day doing something that is making you better.**
- ☐ Study people who have been successful in what you want to do.
- ☐ Research the ins and outs of how to get started and how to sustain yourself doing it.
- ☐ Read and watch videos on everything pertaining to the topic.
- ☐ Find a way to practice doing what you aspire to do.
- ☐ Keep your focus on the work you're doing and not finding an opportunity.

Step 5
Confidence for my moment

> "Fear stifles our thinking and actions. It creates indecisiveness that results in stagnation. I have known talented people who procrastinate indefinitely rather than risk failure. Lost opportunities cause erosion of confidence and the downward spiral begins."
>
> Charles Stanley

This quote sums up the mindset of individuals who are ready, capable and more than qualified but don't believe it. While there are some people who arrogantly jump out of their plane with no parachute, a vast majority of us never feel adequate for the opportunity that is at hand. We're afraid it won't work. We're afraid that we won't be good enough, that we don't know enough, that people won't receive us and some of us are just afraid of the unknown. We won't step up because we're scared of everything that could happen.

When I was in college I had to write a paper on Agoraphobia. While studying on this I found that it is the worst type of phobia a person could have because there is no one thing that you're scared of. People that suffer from this are literally afraid of every potential negative thing that can happen. They normally confine themselves to their homes because they're too terrified of the limitless possibilities of harm that could come their way.

This illness paralyzes your life solely based off of what you think "might" happen. Does this sound familiar to you? I am not suggesting that any of you suffer from Agoraphobia simply because you haven't stepped into the life you desire, I just want you to see how fear of the unknown will keep you from what you know you want. That is why we need confidence. This type of fear cannot exist where there is confidence.

This is the final step in your beating your TRAP. I assume that you have already identified your "More" in you and in the world. That you have recognized what needed to be changed in your life and corrected it. Lastly, that you took advantage of the period between where you were and where you want to be to prepare yourself for this time. If you know what you want, have changed what was keeping you from it and prepared the best you could then there is no reason to be frightened by this moment.

If you wanted to start your own business and you took all the necessary precautions in doing so, don't let your dream die because you have cold feet, open your business. If you were working on being forgiving and you have dealt with all your issues and cleansed yourself of the toxic feelings that stir up anger, don't avoid the person that hurt you the most, go and tell them you forgive them. It doesn't matter if it's a character issue or a desired lifestyle change, you won't see any transformation until you are put to a test. It is often said when you pray to God for patience He won't miraculously put it in you, He'll put you in positions where you need to use it. The same principle applies here.

Now is the time that your transformation should be visible. It will only be visible if you're exercising it and it will only be exercised if you believe in yourself. As an individual that has gone through and has trusted in this process, I believe in you if you have also. If you have put in the work that I asked of you in the first three chapters, I am completely confident in your success. I'm confident without even meeting you because I know these principles work. One sure way to help boost your confidence in yourself is to look back at how you were and see how much you've grown.

Sometimes when we live in the moment we can't see how much better we've become. It's like when you're working out or on a diet; the people that don't see you everyday see a huge change but it's hard for you to see it until you look at an old picture next to a new one. In order to build the confidence needed, you need to compare an old image of you with a current one. When you really look at the contrast it will make you more comfortable in stepping out.

Looking back over each step of the process and each accomplishment you made, will subconsciously build confidence. When you compare your old thinking with your new thinking or your old friends with your new friends, it will show you that you are not in the same space you were before. Some time ago you might not have been ready for this but since you've done what you were supposed to, you are now ready. The truth is you will never see how ready you are until you step out. What you have the capacity to do will always be mystery before you do it. Don't let that mystery be a hindrance, let it be a challenge and take it head on.

There was a time when I was a serial debater. I mean I would be on social media post until the comments got into the hundreds. I would be out arguing for hours about almost anything. I lived to argue. After realizing that debating everything wasn't the best trait that I possessed, one year, I decided to give up debating for Lent. For those 40 days I purposely avoided debates every day. By the time Lent was over, without noticing, I had changed drastically. I didn't notice it until over a year later when someone attempted to argue with me and I passed on the opportunity. I thought to myself "Wow I've changed because before, I would have gone head on with them."

Recognizing the drastic change put me in a position where I felt I didn't have to avoid certain conversations anymore. Avoiding them didn't show I was changed, it just showed I stayed away. What showed that I had changed was joining those conversations and giving my opinion without it turning into an argument. There was a period where avoidance was necessary for me to grow but once I grew I had to trust myself to go back into the same places where my character flaw was brought out and show that I was no longer that person.

I truly believe if you took the time to go through everything we've discussed thus far that you are ready for your opportunity. What I do not believe is that you are ready simply because you sat down and read this book. This is just information; in order for you to be ready you must have applied the principles and as I've stated, some of these take weeks and some years. This is a process not a quick fix. However, if you have gone through the entire process, trust the knowledge and experience you've attained throughout its duration because they have equipped you for this occasion.

Grab a hold of this. Fear is an intangible emotion that cannot be seen; on the other hand, your preparation is something that not only have you touched, you've witnessed it make you better.

Which of these two is more logical for you to follow regarding your life's future? Will you go back to the life you wanted to get away from because of an unproven feeling or move forward knowing that you have followed steps that have proven themselves to you? I suggest the latter.

When you find yourself falling into fear, revisit your steps and allow them to make you feel comfortable. In step three you were supposed to get around some people that were like minded. As the feeling of fear creeps in, go to those individuals so they can help reassure you of your capabilities. If you really have surrounded yourself with the right people, not only will they cheer you on to motivate you, they will give you tips on how they have or are conquering their

5 Steps to Beating the Trap

fears. Having a support group provides a sense of security to help you be confident.

Sometimes the only thing we need to push us over the edge into self confidence is knowing that someone believes in us. That is why having the right people around you is so important because their belief in you can persuade you to believe in you. Think of a time where you or someone you were around was scared to do something but their friends kept telling them they could do it. These instances all tend to have the same phrase uttered by the individual who was in despair: "Ya'll really think I can do it?"

All of the fear and unbelief begins to dissipate for that person due to the belief of the people around them. Once they see others believe in them, the action that follows is normally them doing whatever they were afraid of. In moments of doubt, get around those people who will push you. They have objectively witnessed and been a part of your change. They don't see what you see that is making you fearful; all they see is your potential. Allow what they see to help you be confident enough to see it yourself.

Also in step three you were supposed to put yourself in better environments that will inspire you because what? "If it doesn't inspire you, it's planting a negative thought." If you have made those areas a part of your daily life, when you're feeling unsure, go back to those places. Find what inspired you or showed you what was possible for you to attain. If it showed you it was possible once, it will show you again. One of the biggest mistakes we make is once we start to step out on our dreams, we no longer stay around the places that previously motivated us. We isolate and confine ourselves to the details of what we're attempting to accomplish and lose sight of what drove us to do so.

I've heard rappers who have made money and moved out the hood talk about having to go back in order to be in touch enough to make the music that the people loved them for. In this case the rapper isn't confident in the music they make unless they go back to its place of origin. If you don't feel confident right now, spend some time in those places where your dream originated. Being in the place where the possibilities were discovered will show you how possible it is for you to achieve your goal and seeing them will help you stay confident.

This is your time. You have rid yourself of everything that was related to failure. The things you've forced yourself to do and the things you've forced yourself to let go of have put you in a win-win situation. Challenging your thinking, actions, friends and surroundings have taken you to a place where life as you know it has no limits. You have introduced yourself to "More," which was actually the hard part. Attaining it is easy once you know it's there.

I could spend time saying a bunch of good and inspiring things or give you affirmations to say every day which are good and have their place but that's not what I want to do. Those methods can help build confidence but it won't be supported by anything, it will be as intangible as the fear. What I want is for you to trust the work you've done.

Trust that all the changes you've endured have made you better. Trust that all the information you have acquired has equipped you. Trust the guidance you have received from people that are living out or on the way to their dreams. In order to believe in what you can do you have to trust what you have done.

You should have tons of notes and checklists that show you how far you've come. All the confidence you need lies within you getting out of your feelings and properly assessing your growth. Everything that has been done was all for this moment. What you've learned will not fail you. The only way you can fail is if you're too afraid to try. Understand, confidence doesn't get rid of all fear, it tells you that what you fear isn't a real threat.

Confidence measures your skill and preparation with the thing you're afraid of and concludes that your skill is greater than what you fear. Not that you will never have a little fear but that you know the fear isn't true. People often ask me how I got over the fear of speaking in front of large crowds. My answer is always, "I got up and spoke in front of the crowds." I know that I am a dynamic speaker but every time I have to speak I get butterflies in my stomach. The one thing that stops the butterflies is me actually speaking. Once one word comes out my mouth, the butterflies are gone.

What allows me to ignore the fear and speak in front of any size crowd is my confidence in my preparation. I know when I get up to speak that I am knowledgeable on the subject and clear on the message I want to get across. That confidence is what affords me the strength to push past the fear I feel and command my moment on stage. This is your moment, be confident and allow it to push you past your fears.

In the words of Joyce Meyers, **"Do it afraid."**

This is not just your moment, it is a moment that is just for you. You were hand crafted for this opportunity. All of your life's experiences have prepared you for it. Step out and put yourself to the test because your transformation is complete.

You have BEAT THE TRAP!

Checklist

☐ Compare yourself now to how you were to see your growth.
☐ Look over your checklist and see how many connections you've made and how much you've accomplished and learned.
☐ Trust the knowledge and experience you've acquired.
☐ Revisit every step you went through to get where you are.
☐ Talk to the people who you know will encourage you.
☐ Spend time in the places that made you aware of your possibilities.

B. F. Nkrumah

ABOUT THE AUTHOR

B.F. Nkrumah is a native of Philadelphia whose life is dedicated to the mental, emotional, spiritual and financial repairing of the Black psyche due to all of the trauma we have had to endure. For the past twelve years, B. F. has been one of the most sought after speakers, called upon to help Black people shake internalized self hate, redefine themselves, get reconnected to their true core and become the best version of their true selves that they could be.

He is a six time author, a mentor to hundreds, a developer of leaders and he is committed to restoring the psyche of his people to where it was prior to trauma. Whether through his speaking or writing, he exposes people to hidden truths, concepts and systems, with hopes that his words will radically transform the lives of his listeners.

Outside of his professional career, B.F. is hands on in his community. He is the founder of "The Black Captains," a community organization of Black men who patrol the streets of Philadelphia to make the streets safer for its residents.

He is also the founder of programs for young men and women, "The I in King" & "When Kings raise Princesses."

He was nurtured under leadership which taught him "Leaders are the biggest servants." It is with this mindset that causes him to serve others daily.

B. F. Nkrumah

VISIT WWW.BFNKRUMAH.COM
MORE BOOKS FROM B. F. NKRUMAH

Made in the USA
Middletown, DE
08 April 2023

28325141R00066